WEEP TO THE FALLEN SAPLING

Weep to the Fallen Sapling

A collection of poems

by

DONNY BARILLA

Adelaide Books
New York / Lisbon
2021

WEEP TO THE FALLEN SAPLING
A collection of poems
By Donny Barilla

Copyright © by Donny Barilla
Cover design © 2021 Adelaide Books

Published by Adelaide Books, New York / Lisbon
adelaidebooks.org
Editor-in-Chief
Stevan V. Nikolic

For any information, please address Adelaide Books
at info@adelaidebooks.org
or write to:
Adelaide Books
244 Fifth Ave. Suite D27
New York, NY, 10001

ISBN: 978-1-955196-27-7

Printed in the United States of America

To,

The moss and soil where I rest

Contents

...through the thick of the woods, I find my way...

Watching the Charm Fill the Sky

I

Return of the goldfinch, I
Wrestle damp air through my lungs
As I tremble to the charm of the sky.

Loosely, I walk across the grotto and feel the fabric which warms
    me,
Presses against the spread of the fullness of the sun.

Dipped and wrangled in the fine kelp and chill of the pond,
sweetly, I listen to the winds which laugh upon me.

Flavors of an endless forest shrouds me as each roll
of the fallen chestnut and acorn thumbs upon my shoulders and
nest along my black hair.

Tenderly, I walk upon the cedar chips of the nearest trail.

Tracing the thickness of my gentle legs, paused
upon the fine silks of the emerald kelp, I
breath the wooden chips, wildflowers and spread of the heather.

The trembling sweep of the sky chills the moisture of these soaked
    denims
and the pastes of this cotton shirt.

Reach of the ivy, every stem and root licked and sloped
across the deepest tamp of the deepest pocket of the softest soil.

The breath of the mint filled into the travels of my mouth, throat
and lung.

Beyond the reach of the filled, earth ground, press, I leave the
majestic of this forest.

I wept into the deep of the black soil as rain fell upon the twine of
    roots
and softly, I wept upon the depth of the water well.

Upon the quest for the wealthier, richer treasure of the east branch
    of the forest,
I shook free of the water beads as I drank from the cup of the curled
    leaf.

By morning, I chased the patterns of the sun.

Clouds of a fine heather gray fall to the spirit of the meadow,
silky fog suckled upon the sharp spears of grass as the soft mud
flickered tongues of mist, jousting in a pattern.

I took the path which led to the deepest quilts of leaves, fallen
      upon the earth.

The pine trees reached as an arm of victory challenging the sun.

Softly, the sweet breeze tangled with the peach tender rosebush,
I placed the gentle petal upon my tongue
And rose to the sweeping gush of the broad reach of the hillside;
Walls of evergreens slipped along the pounding wind.

The heavy woods hosted maples and the curl of the maple leaves
which come Autumn, gathered in preparation to the beds of the
    earth.

Looking to the gown and thin carpets of the treetops,
I soothed in clusters of parchment and tender colors
as the canvas stood proudly, naked and empty.

The bark covered branches wailed in this reunion to the sweetened
    carvings of antiquity.

I left her, open blouse and hurdled skirt which drifted beneath her
as a fig leaf, spooling upon the soft trickle of the creek.

In this slithering month of August, I place the spring water upon
the wilt of my tongue and slippery forehead and cheeks.

I fall upon the crashing tap of rain
as the onion root trembled by the edge of the sulking water.

The dusts of the maize swept upon the rising sweep of the wind.

I took the heaviest breath and loafed upon these rising doughs
    which
Trembled into the corner, cupboard and duct of my lungs.

She spent a trickling wrap across the patience of my groin;
The cornfield spoke of discussion as the floods came and filled the
    bowl
With thick bread and tremoring wine.

Puzzles, pieces of shards pasted and lay upon the slight bridge of
the forest trail.

The earth slipped quickly as a mosaic and swooned to the
deepening winds;
I passed the sweet patch of mint, softly, I smelled the bloom of
your flesh and the
fullness of your trembling breasts.

Well into the charming fall of the pink of the sky, I writhed upon
you.

Donny Barilla

With a perfect curve, the sloping breast swooned across me as a pouch
trembling in greens, a pouch of the earth.

I felt the moisture upon the posture of the summit;
tender beads of Summer sweat, early morning, clipped and spread
        upon my feet, boots.

I looked from hilltop to the distant reach of the meadow and I
        breathed the fog of the earth.

I wade the edge of the ocean cove and gently wade through the kelp,
I step softly upon the pebbles and the smoothest of rocks.

After reaching the stream which gushed into the nook of the
    oceans pocket and pouch,
I trembled to the reaching glazes of mist which slipped across the
    needles of pine trees.

By nightfall, I leave the suckling passage and quiver my way into
    the woods.

She lay upon the fine silk sheets of the down feather bed,
I dreamt of the golden fields of barley.

Upon the descent of the crescent moon,
I awoke to the dredging colors of navy as the sun began in preparation.

Breathing deeply, I swept and coddled the golden seed.

Prisms fell from the midmorning sky and shattered upon the
    slithering creek.

With the saunter of the long spears of grass, I climbed the steep greens
of the smothered hills which spread and tangled weaves of the
    oldest brook.

I fell upon the bedding of the pine tree as needles covered me in a
    swooning breath.

Well beneath the low dance of the clouds, spreading across the
     skies belly,
I shook to the approach of the rain, fattened drops which paste
     upon the trim
of my tender shirt.

Looking to the wild heather gray, I dashed to the shroud
of the forest, cupped by the curling leaves and the arch of the
     branches.

Breathing the scent of you, I trembled upon your sauces.

The reach of the sky answered as the sweet cover of all slithering spices
which held posture upon the dome.

The woods stapled as an endless garden, I breathed the aromas
which blossomed in the neighboring forest and swept upon me.

Walking with the nakedness of my tamping feet, I gathered
each petal upon each clover and walked to the end of the horizon.

Sweetly, I coddle each thread and speck of dust as the quilts of the
        outside
lay silent and spread in a shroud of perfect white.

The dampness curls upon my neck and tenderly,
I stroke her in the soils of the earth.

Softly, I hear the clatter of her bones as the marrow freezes in the
        slowest motion.

The silent waves of her naked body, shook and trembled across
    the threads
and fabrics which soothed the groin of the speechless earth.

I stroked every nook and cupboard of her pale full flesh.

Softly, I slept upon the dough and tremble of her open breasts.

On the glaze on the open field, I listened to the sting of the
    whistling
flood of Winter's fangs which angled upon me and swept each
    white mound
of the lofting bloom of ice and tossing beds.

I witnessed your face as the snow danced past; gently, I wept upon
    you.

Late Autumn the Sweat Permeates across the Earth

II

The sky opened, this full belly pelted rains upon the sweet grass.
I knelt and angled my mouth to the tapping pearls, puckering
        upon the slowest
moving creek.

By late afternoon, the leaves sheltered upon me in endless tones.
here, alive in the open fields, greens and rise of the scarlet oak
        motioned upon the wind.

I watch the moisture rest upon the curling cup of the defeat of the
    endless leaves
soft and filled with dew, each drops to the threads of the earth.

Clusters of the gathered leaves, I rest by the elm and the tulip tree;
with the fade of the tangled moments, I deepened into the
    chanting bones of the earth.

The evening sky bled through the month of October as I trembled
My chilled fingers upon you and held sweet moisture from the
     scattered
Puddles which leveled across the sparse trees.

I looked to the empty forest and wandered upon the spiny, stiff grass.

Pines stretched from the sloping curve of the mountains well
     upon the depths
far to the north; I stood and watched the cones and needles as they
punctured the earth.

In a moment, I left the maples which I called home.

Into the deepest stretch of Autumn,
I awoke and look upon the heavy forest which rose steep to the west.

This endless dance of the empty woods began a slight coat of
     cotton laid snow
across the crunch of the earth.

I watched the red maple leaves shake and flicker through the
  trembling slant
Of the sun as these pieces of tender Autumn gather across me and
  landed on the forest floor.

Searching for you and our last touch and last gesture, I found the
  earth loosened as the rocks
Swept beneath the mosses and in reverence, the ferns pampered
  above you.

With arms reaching through the falling fog,
I witness this forest, barren and desolate as the fallen leaves
caught a fine, silk breeze and fumbled across the weeping woodlands.

I look upon the willow tree and tremble to the creek where I last
saw you.

The buds pucker four months late;
into the delicate jaws of Autumn, they left months early.

Looking upon the soft, slight dusting of snow,
I slowed and witnessed her blouse loosen and fall upon the cake
      of the earth.
Wind tossed and I gathered her scent in the chasm of my lungs.

The full grass grew as a pattern, coddled by the early Autumn and
    early dash
of the morning flood, spread with dew.

I rest in the wealth of these treasures of the grotto which spoke to me
in fine rebuttal and tender softness.

From here I see the belly of the ocean and I smile upon my brethren,
the wave of the eight islands.

The earth sulked and moaned to the coolest of sober skies.
I wedged through the spice garden and placed my thick hands
upon the dashing light at nightfall.

Quietly, the breeze from the northern hills caressed the fullness of me.

Walking through the fields of wheat, I breathed the fragrance of
    your tender womb.

Gently, I looked across the thin meadow and witnessed the empty
    woods
which trembled to each shaking branch.

I drank from the thin brook and tasted the blood of each marvel
    of the forest.

The sky fractured and shed eager shades of apricot across the wild
roots and reaching spears of green.

Into the soft glazes of the Autumn spread,
I surrendered to the thrashing wind which shook each strand of
    my hair.

I listened to you moan whispers across the gown of the sweetest
    dance of the earth.

The ancient hillside deepened to a dashing breeze of the softness
  of the earliest of October
Moments which hosted the earth toned hues which strapped to
  every branch.

The approaching nakedness of the woods thickened as I heard the
  drums which demanded
From the wilting sky.

Her milk filled breasts slithered from the hills as the grooves
spread from creek to gentle creek.

I drank from her as the water fell and chilled the emptiness of my
parchment throat.

Most tender, I slipped to her in the slowest wave of barley.

The field of morning grass hosted the pearl shaped dew
as each pouch of clover stoods as a sweet taste upon the chalice.

By the enchantment of midday, I relished upon the aroma
of the patch of mint, by afternoon,
I walked near to the onion stalk which threaded into the earth.

The sweat burrowed as driftwood and parted across the bridge of
    my forehead and cheeks.

I removed every fabric of my full body and waded to the waist
    which lulled me to sweep beneath the wild stream and the
    pasted glisten of the chestnut hue of my hair lay perfect
    upon my skull.

Departed into the flicker and dashing sunlight which cluttered
    through the forest trees,
I found the tender hollow and slept in the shatter of the sunlight.

I removed the Fabric, blouse and fleece which coated the earth as
    the earliest
Spread of dusted covering of snow.

With slow moving steps upon the white, thin beds of snow, I
Looked upon the gown of ivory and thought of her as the sweet
    sky rained upon me.

With the brisk shuffle of the billowing sky,
every fallen leaf coddled the shuffling of my feet.

Upon you, the soil, moist and dark, narrowed upon the bone.

Upon the touch of the coolest hands,
I shake as the foams spread upon the wet sands of the ocean.

Looking to the lighthouse, I fall into the heaviest of slumber.

I awaken to the kelp of the ocean deep and burrow within you.

Softly I Loafe Near the Trembling Nest

III

I spoke to the knotted and gnarled branches
which spoke upon return of the loosened pages of the loafing leaves.

The crows nest perched on the canvas of the treetops,
I sank my way between the red maples and the scarlet oak
which filled my lungs with the dashing threads of the woodlands
    breath.

Within the breadth of the forest, I moan,
I remove myself for the slicing burrow of the wealthy stream.

Soft patterns of moss and the regal spread of the ferns
quiver and shift beneath the step of my feet.

I drink deeply and continue further on trails and paths.

I wept to the song of the blackbird as soothing rain brought
a chill across my neck and the sulking broadness of my shoulders.

Here, in the fractured tangerine glazes of the sky,
each bird took passage upon the flooding winds.

Swiping my thick fingers upon the curling leaf, I tasted the broth
of the ocean and creek.

I search for the trail which caresses the silky grasses rising
across the rolling hilltops, tender and aware as the turkey vulture
spread upon the groove of the earth with width and shadow.

Reaching camp, I wash in the soot and thick smoke of the fumbling
    fire.

Alive in the hot springs, I soaked in the brew of the earth,
peaked and trembling from beneath each heavy crust.

Swabbed in the nakedness of the woods which surround me,
I clothed and stood upon the mountain peak as endless dancing,
    thin branches

Marveled upon the long shadows of Winter passage.

Into the jousting spears, this sweet Summer grass,
I listened to the insects which burrow in the fragrance of the soil
which carves tenderly beneath me.

I witness the flight of the male cardinal as the seeds
snap and flood the mouths of the hue a deeper brown.

Donny Barilla

Here, the cabin speaks with the tread of the naked foot.

With the nimble pry of my strengthening fingers,
I remove the satin curve and curl of the blouse,
soft in all abandonment.

I tremble upon each lofting flicker of dust.

I faced the most southern reach and watched the slicing 'v'
of the Canadian geese find distribution to the quilted north,
alive in this softening pasture.

I stood upon the sheer face of the smooth rock,
well perched and broadened with the carpets of heavy green moss.

I slung my eyes into the canal which ushered forth the slithering
branch of driftwood and fumbling leaves.

By nightfall, I stood surrounded by the thickest of woods.

Here, in the wellspring of morning youth,
clouds fell upon me as the finest mist bled from every stitch of fog.

I listen to the pinecones tamping upon the beds of crisp needles
and crackle of the branches of the hickory tree
flexing upon the heaviest wind.

Wrapped in furs and the thickest boots,
I entered the fangs of this trembling woods, gripped by the fangs
    of Winter.

Blankets sweeping in the spread of the white snow mounds,
I speak to the fumbling clouds reaching across the sky.

Along the ravine on the hilltop, I heard the 'caw' of the trembling
    murder of crows.

I rest in stillness by the calm Summer pond.

The kelp wrapped through toes and across the wedge of my ankles;
every bead of pearl shaped sweat trickled across my temples and cheeks.

With the rising heat of the sun,
I watched as she fell slick upon the cottons of her shirt.

I sink my teeth into the rhythms and juice of the plums.
Tenderly, I open my shirt and vest upon the swabbing, cool winds.

You approach me in the shadows of evening
as the starlings pronounce victory with the scattered rest of seed
     and pod.

Snow melted across the naked spread of the hillside,
I felt the warmth of the rise of Spring.

I stood with all residue of emptiness as the first
bud snapped into the sundance and freshness of the mumbling air.

I walk beneath the blossoms of the cherry tree
as soft pink petals rest upon the bridge of my shoulders
and tangle through the long fullness of my hair.

Into the distance, I speak of the soft lake and all trembling water.
The willow tree answers in the slow dance of this kin.

I stand by the groaning width of the suckling waves of the lake;
Trembling by the pebbled edge, I wedge my feet and wade.

Sauces fill in the cloudy sky as seagulls thread through the
    moisture of the air
And tenderly, I breath the softest posture of clutter of the
    warming sun.

Donny Barilla

I remove myself from the forest and all crimping beds of leaves.

Questing, I search the southern lancing mountain
and in quiet gesture; he greets me for the water of the trickling spring.

As I reach this peak, soaked in dripping fog,
I sweetly lose my way.

I pause, trembling feet steep among the soaked, jade colored grass.

Breathing the scents as the earth rises and speaks of Spring
and all spreading pregnancy,
I reach the scarlet oak and sleep to the music of the wrestling branches.

Droplets perch across the soft gathering of the tiger lily.
I walk through the softness of the pale colored house.
Each thread of the pine tree bathes in the blanche of the sun.

Standing before the bay window, I shake the locks before the heavy
draft.

On the sandy crest of the flaring brine,
opened from the pulse of the gushing waves of the tender sea,
I hear the egrets pamper through the softest prism of the sun.

Swollen with deepening clouds, gentle fog trembles
across the flare of the floundering birds, moving in the pasture
of the motions of the salted deep.

Refresh to the Flavors of the Treasures of the Woods

III

I step upon the wild girth of the thin pasture
Which threads through the moans of the branches of the pines
and spruces.

With the crunch and snap of my retort,
I crush the pinecone and hurry along.

Past the flooding creek and into the rise of the emerald hills
Which tend the seeded breath of air and quiver to the wind,

I lather my feet, soft and naked as the soils of the trembling sky
Swell and unburdone before me.

Roots spread as deepened fangs thrusted deeply into the earth;
I breathed the flesh of my ancestors as the swift current of the wind
broomed and glazed across me.

WIth the slight gesture of the tree branches, gnarled and shaking
     with crackling
antiquity, I walked further into the breast of the earth.

I reached the crowded hush of the willow trees.
I listened to each branch and pod as a language not yet understood.

The sky fell in a clouded smash of mourning rain and I flooded
upon the cupped, curling leaves which drizzled each pouch of rain.

Donny Barilla

The crab apple tree shook every branch and scattered the earth
with motionless food for soil and rested upon the thin, jade grass.

I tugged the passing breath of the fallen cloak of the sky;
moments passed, I drank the tapping rain as they softened the
     coarseness
of my full hair and cotton shirt.

Near her, I rest upon the clusters of well spread leaves which
caress in the bosom of this Autumn nakedness and this shedding
     fleece.

With every dance of the trembling moonlight which flickered
soft blues and silvers through the limbs and branches of the trees,

I motioned closely and kissed the fullness of her lips.

Near her, I rest upon the clusters of well spread leaves which
caress in the bosom of this Autumn nakedness and this shedding
    fleece.

With every dance of the trembling moonlight which flickered
soft blues and silvers through the limbs and branches of the trees,

I motioned closely and kissed the fullness of her lips.

Standing upon the sloping forests, I witness
the shades of the Autumn gown, fading in tans, yellows, browns
    and lighter browns,
loafing dust shroud of the approach of the emptiness of Winter.

Evenings pass evenings and I wade through the icy chill of the tender
white mounds which wrap and tug upon the trunk glaze the reaching
    branch.

The earth warmed to the slant of the rising sun.
Quietly, fog lifted, trembled as the smoke of the chanting of my
	brethren.

I waded through the thick of the dewdrops which perched upon the
	silent leaves;
by nightfall, I soaked in the spreading mist which fell from the
	tunneling
dash of the fallen cloud.

I stood by the spiny reach of the aspen tree,
soft buzzing wind threaded the branch and blossom.

Here, on the glaze on the mountaintop, I breath the aromas of the
    downward valley
which rises with wheat as the breads of the earth.

In this forest majestic, here, the polished branch of the willow tree
sweats beads of dew which coils in impartiality
and trembles to the dry cakes of the earth.

Upon reaching the dry curve of the defeated stream,
I weep to each thicket and thorn.

I opened my mouth to the wild fumble of the breathing, moaning
    creek.
I drank heavy and filled
my body with treasures and full droplets of the pearl bead.

The sky gushed across me and sweet felt of the peach rosebush
motioned and sweetened upon the sliver of tongue and cheek.

Donny Barilla

Weaving trail of the sauntering forest reaches before me
in the cast of pebbles and rocks and the sweep of the cedar chips.

I breath the map of the bark and trunk which deplete
from the thin wooden paper which falls upon the forest floor
which shadows sweetly from last Spring.

I reach the crossroads of the needles spread upon the grooves of
    the pine floor.
Looking west, I smell, see the dying plains.

I lust at the icy capped mountains to the north.
I hear the trembling gush of the ocean to the east.
Behind me I shake to the trembling woods.

Donny Barilla

The drifting clouds stitched pulses of slapping rain
as the low sweeping clouds of heather gray
trembled upon the breasted, fullness of the sweetest hills.

Here, I rest upon the nakedness of the wealth of the earth.

.

I wrapped in the shroud and suckled upon the fine moisture
which shook me as I rest upon the crest beneath the earth.

Gentle gales trembled across me as the flickering grass
whispered the secrets of the shadows of the earth.

Softly, I relish in the covenant of this soil and marrow of the bone.

I spoke to the phantom in the deepest pocket of the writhing forest. Endless vapors rose from the dancing leaves and clung to the staleness of the green pond.

I stood upon the scattered boulders as the wind from the north caught and shuffled my hair.

From the kitchen window of the thick cabin,
I softened my eyes as the aroma of the rising bread filled me
in the approaching Winter.

She leaned, reached her thick arms in the oven trap
as I moaned the softest groan to the fullness of her breasts.

Clover, the patch of mint, threaded across the silks of the meadow.

Upon reaching the scarlet oak, I trembled with the passages of the
tender breeze.

I stood, stopped at the crossing trails and found the treasure
of the jasper and the youth of the black slate.

Swiftly, I return to the bushes and thicket of this heavy wood.

She shook the fabrics and threads from her full body as the
     cutting Winter wind
grieved with the freeze of the softness of her black, long hair.

With the burn of my groin, I watched as she fell upon the icy earth
and welded to the dead sweetly.

I watched the crows approach in the perfect measure.

From the Coddling Earth I Rise

IV

Into the earth, placed upon the satin vault,
I explore the winds and the tapping rains, greens of the meadow
and the shine of the smashing sun.

I feel the vapor shroud across me as I nurse to the edge
of every rippling lake.

From the finest mahogany lumber, I feel and smell the polish.
Tenderly, I once stepped across the moist beds of grass
as the snapping wind grew swift and demanding.

I return to the vessel of my growth in the womb
and reach my arms across the brine and above the pounding rain.

Donny Barilla

The red maple held the leaf
midway through the weeping scars of Winter.

I paused above the stretching roots
and breathed the heat of my lungs, soft and humid.

With a dash, the curled, crimped piece fell upon the layers of snow.

The gem of the earth welcomed me in shards,
a perfect trim which motioned my soft distortion
to the sketches of the soil and earth.

Upon reaching revival, I shatter to the tremble of this mosaic.

I threaded this path to the garden deep,
swabbed in the flourish of the coolest waters,
alive, the kelp and well measured soot.

Thrashing in the depth of this heavy floods which grip me
in the volumes of approaching rest.

Listening through the soil of the carpets and threads which fasten
    to the earth,
I listen to the crackling of her bones as she pronounced
a tender quake and quiver and shook beneath the mud from the
    pounding rain.

Lathers on the roof of the earth
tremble marrow upon the edge of my yearning tongue.

Donny Barilla

I spoke upon the loafing spindles of the seasoned breeze.

Softly, I touched her, closed her eyes,
I closed my eyes and dreamed of the river styx.

With the passage of time, I swept the dust from each corner and
tread of the earth.

She craved the chalk, dust and marrow of the rib of the sweet soil
of the tender enriched passage in the breads of the earth.

Walking home, I paused at the grotto and grove which hosted
the floods of the pounding welts from the rain.

I hear her writhe in the soil beneath the crust and cakes.

Walking upon the crumbling leaves of the Autumn forest,
I motion these boots across the burgundy and tans of the eager flood
of the woodland floor.

October's fragrance moves and chymes upon the flesh of my arms
and the bust and threads of my hair. From distance becoming
      arrival, the chapel
tosses each sliver of sandalwood.

I lay beneath the moss and the stretch of sweet motioning clovers;
I breath the cool chill of the earth.

Awaiting the reunion of my ancestors and my brethren and my fellows,
I sweep and fall to the deepest of slumbers as the wind
tosses and casts me in parcels upon the tender hillside.

I reach through the minerals of the thick soil;
I arrive in the ocean, forest and crest of the hilltop.

Pollens fumble across me as the slicing wind shakes me in
      fragments and loosens this nesting.

Breathing every dash of air, I rise to your summit and perfect flesh.

I shook the resting slope of buds of my shoulders and
eagerly witnessed the burial of this green groove of Spring.

Every snapping pod which once rested upon the elm, black hickory
        and the tangled buds
of the aspen tree groomed the bride of the most tender earth.

Precisely, one year from now, I witness the small, green buds of the
        willow tree.

Crouching on the ledge of the peak of this empty mountaintop,
save ice and mounds of powdered white snow,

I look upon the deep of the thickest forest,
I hunger for the birchwood and shards of the cedar.

By nightfall, I fasten my eyes and frosted body upon the glazes of
the earth.

I wade through the tall stretching grass and breath the scent
of the onion root as the clover rest humble and filled with treasures.

Here, early Spring, the cup and curl of the leaf hosts the beads of
     the droplet,
alive in the thread of morning.

I breath each fragrance of the earth as the glen and meadow step
     upon me.

The twisting trail pressed eagerly through the thorn bushes
and wild twitch of the burrs and glory of the aloe,
I reached the posture of the pines which thinned and loosened the
      fall
of the needles.

I met you in the soft mud and tender moss upon the wedge of the
      open path.
The winds softly wept across me.

In flesh, I moan to this prison;
the shatter of the rib and I twitch in grasses upon the breasts of the
      earth.

Tenderly, I suckle to the pastes of the snap of the marrow
as the sweeping stream brews upon the nakedness of my body and
      shroud.

I stood in the flickering fog of the garden and meadow,
coiling across her, she departed from the garment and holstered
the scent of the forest and patch of mint.

Moments passed, I drift to the spirits of the trembling wind.

Nine slopes, the curve of the southern hilltops
trembled their soft grass upon the dash of the swift winds.

Gently, I tread the wavering touch of the grass writhing in full bloom;
I reach the stream where I once was lost and tore through the
      descending
motions of the sweeping blackbirds.

I dredge through the thin roots of the pouches of gleaming grass.

Softly, the wildflower petal tosses and nests upon the tangling spears.

I sulk in the moisture of the fields and meadows as the sky weeps
upon me.

I rest in the arms and lap of the moaning Autumn branches
which chant the mist and vapors of my departed flesh and
caress me in these trembling leaves.

In a last glance of the breast of the fullest moon,
I grow as sap upon the threads of the earth.

With the Snap of the Bud Seeds Roam across the Fields

IV

I move through the wealthy meadow and cling to the ripe, moisture
    of the grass.
By nightfall, I soften my flesh to the tap of the trembling rain.

Sweeping gales tickle the treetops with fullness and finger and thumb.
Pausing at the threaded arm of the creek, I drink the gushing spring
And return to the stretching fields.

Near the quivering arms of the wheat, I tremble at this reaching touch.
Washed in the seed of the tans and golden fields, I lather to the
    open pry of dust.

Wild winds thrash across the heavy crunch and stampede
Which stays beneath me in an unrequited loafe where lusts fall
    upon me.

Turning to fields edge and I taper across the field and rest at the
    foot of the woodlands.

With trembling lust,
the gazelle dashed across the thinning grass and strewn
fumbling rock of the tan and golden plains.

I broadened my chest and breathed with a Winter cloak,
the descending sky.

Walking the creeks edge into the pine forest
resting upon the ancient child of the earth,
I spoke to the slapping spring and softened upon the wellspring of
      this birth,
food of the forest and carriage of the trembling leaves.

Upon the perch, sadalled on the thin wavering tree limb,
I breathed to the opening flower which months later showered the
    earth in petals.

I swept and motioned along the pebbles and wood chips of the trail;
Upon reaching the crest of the threaded hill,

I swam through every fragrance and spiced scent.

Soft flavors rushed through the stream which spoke
of change and enhancement.

I drank, waded with nakedness along the chill of the spirited gush.

By nightfall, I breached the wrapping arms of Spring.

I listened to the moans as the slapping wind threshed through the
    trees
and sudden trembling sliced in the madness of the earth.

Summer flew upon a crooked twist as the heavy breath of Autumn
softened and painted the forest floor.

I reach across her and crumble in the rise of the dough;
sweetly, her scents of the fullest breasts swell inside of me.

From ribs to abdomen, I hold with a murmur and tremble
as the flower, I open to the linens and fleece, I cup this chalice in my
    palm.

Dust floods the room as each facet and limb moans in rhythms
    and chants.

I deepen these fangs and teeth with the seeping suckle upon the peach and pear.

As you wrap yourself in your arms, I retreive you in jams and the
glades which
soothe and sweep overhead.

In the posture of the sweat of your forehead and breast, I glisten
through you.

Shred of the bark of the birchwood
gathered upon the floor of the woodland stretch.

Nestled seeds of the surrounding hyacinth took flight;
I stepped to the cove of the ocean floor and listened to the pilgrimage
as the white birch wept to the cedars and scarlet oak.

Soothing and swift, each loafing pollen tapered
grasses and ferns which thread the floor of the roaming woods.

In the girth of the full popping buds,
I breathed the scent of the sweetest flavors which swept across me
    and filled me.

Into the arms of mid Spring, I fell and kissed the flickering green leaves.

She swam through the deepened channel of the bed
of the groove in the edge of the fullness where the lake holds posture.

I smiled upon the nakedness of her sweetest pale flesh.
the full cap of her pasted hair gleamed as chestnuts;
I place my hands upon her and fade to the prism of the rising sun.

In Winter, I wail and curl to the drip of the dying sun;
I watch as the sky bleeds burgundy and whimpers upon the horizon's
    ledge.

Now Spring and I wash my feet in the glazes of the grass covered field.

With a brief moment, I recall this place.

.   •

Removed from the womb of the earth,
I walk across fresh moisture of the floor of the meadow.

Now, I reach the heavy scent of the scarlet oak as leaves
wrap across the seasoning of the breath arriving from the thick
rolling hilltops.

I swim through the fragrance of the tenderness of the thickest
parcel of the wilderness where the woods soothed in sap and lumber.

In the deepness of late Spring,
I found and trembled upon the slight quiver of the well spread
      patch of mint.

I spoke into the oven of the earth
which warmed the breads and creams as the pine trees writhed and
      shouted

sweet moans of the choir of this whipping breeze through the leaves.

Now morning, the sun splintered
into the crest and shone reds and navies upon the horizon.

Donny Barilla

Past the wedged, group of meadows,
I entered the soft floor and tall, treasured trees
as they hosted laughter as it danced through the leaves.

I felt the wood chips fondle the arch of my feet,
softly, I looked upon the full open buds as the trembling breeze
walked through the mumbling glen.

The sun trembled in prisms as the light flickered across the sea.

Gently, I wade through the foams and kelp which caress my ankle
and foot.
Along the bath in the spread of the water, I shake the heavy brine
loose
as the dancing colors of the coral reef thickens in the deep stretch
and channel.

Looking to the seagulls of the starving wind, each 'caw' moans in
perfect rhythm.

She slid across me and prepared me in fragrance and each of the
    desperate spices.
Looking across the pale slope of her shoulders, I watch the saffron sky
open and engulf the sweet caress of the horizon.

Months passed, I swell within her as the fluids of cream thicken in
    her breast.

The meadow upholds me as I walk through the deep
suspension of the seed and burrow and thorn.

With the deep step of these boots, the pollens
loosen and carve their way to the trembling gush of wave and breeze.

From the Deep of Night Shadows Climb the Wall

V

I arise from this satin bed, cloaked in shades of ivory.
I listen to the growling moans of my people
As the light fades to blackness.

Well stood, I walk through the grotto as the moisture of the grass
Anoints me in the thickest beads.

Softness of the downward thrust of the sky
swept across me and licked the edges of my fine chestnut hair
as the sands preserved and coddled me in sweet breath of the
      falling clouds,
I taste the fluids of night.

I yearn to the lusts of the salted water;
I carve my way through the beds of the soil of the deep of the soothing
      sea.

I slipped and slithered across the blue gems and ices
of the fluids of her sunken abdomen as the sting of her eyes
howl a distant cry.

I shake across her as the shadows lather across her chill and flesh.

With opened eyes, I saunter within the shadows
which reach and climb the tender and smooth face of the wall.

Along the tender sloping arch of the bridge,
I sweeten to the moss and ancient touch of the heavy glen
where I sleep and slouch upon the sweetened breeze.

Donny Barilla

With the fangs of the farthest reach of sleek Winter night
I stood, shook the silent branches of the trees.

I trembled through the mounds of the white snow of this carving
    spread and quilt.

Moment passed and I fall
to dust as the fleck of blackbirds as they swim the ivory cloak of
    the sky.

Days stretch to a long Summer pause.
I sleep at the gnarled hook of the oak tree as leaves muffle and shake.

By the end of the farthest year at the end of the farthest day,
I soften and depart into the richest soil of glen, field and meadow.

In the carving hour of night, I slither upon the flickering, drowsy
    hours of dark.

Unaware, we walked through the woods which sang as a symphony
And shook the leaves upon the crisp grass which slithered in perch
of the bead.

Here, the pond where we met, I knelt and trace my forefinger
across the green kelp.

Gently, I turn to her and she fell upon the dust of the wind.

I feel the sweat which rose from the pounding heat of the rising sun.
I removed the fibers and threads of this garment
as each suckling verb danced upon the hyacinth and the wealth of
    the aspen tree.

By the hours of night, I wrestled upon the casket of soil and grass.

Casting a long glance, I melded to the moistures of the shadow of
    night
which stemmed upon the sweet flavors of honey and sap,
a quiver in the dances of this forest.

I pause within this hollow and I hear the dampness of the sweetest
    dew,
dropping upon the cakes of the earth.

Well into the black of the starving woods,
I reached a thick pasture where the plums withered and soothed me
In the greatest of temptation.

I speak of the thickening of the rivers edge.
Powders of the sweet Autumn wildflowers tangle upon me
as the reaching depth of the softest soil suckles my ankles and boots.

Arrival at the trail, I swim through the haze of the snap of the buds
as I sweep across the level of the forest floor.

Sauces of the heat of this craving bite of Summer,
walking through the thickets and thorns pepper me with blood.

Alone with this starvation and alone with the nakedness
of the empty creek which now breathes upon the air,

I feel the crackling chalks and empty marrow of my bones.

Here in the empty woods, slung with white beds of snow,
I listen to the earth and hear the vowels of sweet temptation
as the crows flood this icy floor.

A moist reunion of blood and borrowed flesh
deepen to the cage where we live.

Posture of the tall grass holds gems in the sliver of the spear
as the smallest chalice of the clover speaks in names of the spirit.

Heat of this dash of Summer, floods upon the sloping hills and the
    distant
stretch of the meadows, fields and waves of wheat and barley.

Moments passed, I walk through the fields in vapors and haze.

Donny Barilla

By the bank of the rise of the gushing river,
I felt the sweet sauces of the pine and maple.

Brown floods of the edge, I wept as the veins of the house of these
woods,
I tremble to the beds of nesting needles and join her in the depths
of the earth.

I fasten my grip to the water well as the loafing leaves dash upon the posture of my shoulders and my fine hair.

I feel the age in the dust and chalk of my bones.

In a scurry and swift reach, I hear the moaning press of the wind as the scent of the earth calls me.

Into the snare of the Summer heat,
I trembled my jaws upon the twig of the maple tree.

Softly, I deepen into the breads of the earth.

I recall her, filled with life and full of nakedness.
I recall her as moist and sweet with an eager tremble.

Within the shadow on the wall, I rest upon the pouches filled with
    creams
As she heaved a bead covered breast.

Now, I lust into the tremor of the shavings of this flesh.

Late Autumn and the trees have lost their color.
I speak to the thousand bones which clutter to the sweeping rain.

Into the solitude of the empty forest,
I breath the fragrance of the wilted and bruised.

Here, I cling to the rib of the soils beneath these patterned grasses.

Here, I depart to the jades and emeralds of the trembling woods.
Walking upon the earth and the softest soils,
I hear the breath of you as the fields before you rise in loafing dust.

At forest edge, I quiver to the endless scents which croon across me.

...here, I tremble upon the dying bush as the wind carries me in dust...

About the Author

Under and within the landscape of nature, Donny Barilla coats the palate of his metaphoric and imagist reach as he uses the tremble of his pen to wrangle upon the fever of his surroundings which flood and weave each page. Donny motions primarily as a poet and uses techniques such as he writes books of short stories and novellas and searches his creativity in multiple arenas fastened through thought provoking paints which slip from word to page to book. Keeping late hours which sometimes bleeds into the rising patterns of the sun, he works in his study keeping an espresso machine close at hand. Here, he allows the softened press of his discipline, awake and aware at each moment. Having placed ninety-four poems in journals and magazines, he also donated twenty three books to libraries, academic and public. Donny took first place in the Adelaide Literary Award for Poetry and has placed on two other occasions. After building a construct of vowels and consonants, the words blend upon the page as he pays due respect to the motions of the English language and passions of poetic touch.

Made in the USA
Middletown, DE
23 October 2021

50285962R00092